Copyright Law
Publishers

A Comprehensive G

Published August 2025

First Edition

© By: Paige Hargis

Disclaimer: This book provides general information about copyright law for educational purposes only. It is not legal advice. Copyright law is complex and varies by jurisdiction. For specific legal questions or concerns, consult with a qualified intellectual property attorney.

Table of Contents

Introduction

Chapter 1: Copyright Fundamentals

Chapter 4: International Copyright Considerations

Chapter 5: Using Others' Work in Your Book

Chapter 6: Protecting Your Work from Infringement

Chapter 7: Copyright Issues Specific to KDP

- Metadata and copyright information
  - Publication date
  - Author name and contributors
  - ISBN information
- Territorial rights and distribution
  - Territorial rights selection
  - Copyright enforcement across territories
  - Translation rights
- Content updates and copyright implications
  - Copyright date for updated works
  - Notifying existing customers
  - Version tracking
- Rights reversion and termination
  - Removing your book from KDP
  - KDP Select termination
  - Rights after termination
- Account termination and copyright issues
  - Rights after account termination
  - Proving ownership after termination
  - Appealing account termination
- Copyright disputes on KDP
  - Infringement reporting process
  - Responding to infringement claims

Copyright Law for Self-Publishers: A Comprehensive Guide

Introduction

As a self-published author for example on (KDP) platform, you've taken control of your publishing journey. You've crafted your manuscript, designed your cover (or hired someone to do it), formatted your book, and navigated the KDP dashboard to bring your creation to market. But amid all these tasks, have you given proper attention to one of the most crucial aspects of publishing: copyright law?

Understanding copyright law isn't just a legal formality—it's an essential part of protecting your creative work and your livelihood as an author. In the traditional publishing world, publishers typically handle copyright matters. As a self-publisher, this responsibility falls squarely on your shoulders.

Why Copyright Matters for Self-Publishers

Copyright law serves several vital functions for authors:

1. Protection of your creative work: Copyright law gives you exclusive rights to reproduce, distribute, display, and create derivatives of your work.

2. Financial security: By controlling who can use your work and under what conditions, you protect your ability to earn income from your creative efforts.

3. Creative control: Copyright ensures that you decide how your work is used, adapted, or modified.

4. Legal recourse: If someone uses your work without permission, copyright law provides the legal framework for addressing the infringement.

The digital age has made copyright more important than ever. With a few clicks, your eBook can be copied, shared, and distributed worldwide—sometimes legally, sometimes not. Understanding copyright law helps you navigate this landscape confidently.

What This Guide Covers

This comprehensive guide will walk you through everything you need to know about copyright law as it applies to self-publishing on KDP. We'll cover:

- The fundamentals of copyright law and what it protects
- How and when to register your copyright
- Creating an effective copyright page for your book
- International copyright considerations for global sales
- Using others' work in your book legally
- Protecting your work from infringement
- KDP-specific copyright issues and policies
- Special considerations for different types of books
- Copyright for co-authored works and collaborations
- Common copyright myths and misconceptions

Whether you're publishing your first book or your fiftieth, this guide will help you understand and navigate copyright law with confidence.

How to Use This Guide

This guide is designed to be both comprehensive and practical. Each chapter builds on the previous one, but you can also jump to specific sections that address your immediate concerns.

Throughout the guide, you'll find:

- Practical examples that illustrate key concepts
- Sample templates you can adapt for your own use
- Step-by-step instructions for processes like copyright registration
- Tips and best practices from experienced self-publishers
- Resources for further learning and assistance

While this guide provides valuable information about copyright law, it's important to note that it does not constitute legal advice. Copyright law can be complex, and laws vary by country. For specific legal questions or concerns, consult with an intellectual property attorney.

Let's begin our journey through copyright law for self-publishers, starting with the fundamental concepts you need to understand.

Chapter 1: Copyright Fundamentals

Before diving into the specifics of copyright for self-published books, it's essential to understand what copyright is, what it protects, and how it works. This chapter covers the fundamental concepts that form the foundation of copyright law.

What Is Copyright?

Copyright is a form of intellectual property protection granted by law to creators of original works. It provides the creator with exclusive rights to use, reproduce, distribute, display, and create derivative works based on the original creation.

The U.S. Copyright Office defines copyright as "a type of intellectual property that protects original works of authorship as soon as an author fixes the work in a tangible form of expression."

In simpler terms, copyright is a legal mechanism that:

- Recognizes you as the creator of your work
- Gives you control over how your work is used
- Allows you to benefit financially from your creative efforts
- Provides legal recourse if someone uses your work without permission

Copyright is not a single right but rather a bundle of exclusive rights that include:

1. Reproduction right: The right to make copies of your work
2. Distribution right: The right to sell, rent, lease, or lend copies of your work
3. Public display right: The right to show your work publicly
4. Public performance right: The right to perform your work publicly
5. Derivative works right: The right to create new works based on your original work

As a self-published author, understanding these rights helps you make informed decisions about how your book is used and distributed.

What Does Copyright Protect?

Copyright protects "original works of authorship" that are fixed in a tangible medium of expression. For authors, this includes:

- Literary works (novels, short stories, poems, etc.)
- Non-fiction works (biographies, textbooks, articles, etc.)
- Compilations and collective works
- Dramatic works and accompanying music
- Pictorial, graphic, and sculptural works (including book illustrations)

What copyright does NOT protect:

- Ideas, concepts, principles, or methods (only the expression of these)
- Titles, names, short phrases, and slogans (these might be protected by trademark law instead)
- Facts, news, or data (though the specific expression or arrangement of facts may be protected)
- Works in the public domain
- Works not fixed in a tangible form (such as an improvised speech that isn't recorded)

Example: Ideas vs. Expression

Let's say you have an idea for a novel about a detective who solves crimes using time travel. The general idea of a time-traveling detective is not protected by copyright. Anyone can write a story with this premise.

However, once you write your specific story with unique characters, plot developments, and narrative style, that particular expression of the idea is protected by copyright. Another author cannot copy your specific characters, dialogue, or plot sequences without permission.

When Does Copyright Protection Begin?

One of the most important things for self-publishers to understand is that copyright protection is automatic. Your work is protected by copyright from the moment it is created and fixed in a tangible form that is perceptible either directly or with the aid of a machine or device.

In practical terms, this means:

- Your manuscript is protected as you write it
- You don't need to publish the work for it to be protected
- You don't need to register the copyright for protection to exist
- You don't need to use the copyright symbol (©) for protection (though it's still recommended)

While registration is not required for copyright protection to exist, registering your copyright with the U.S. Copyright Office (or equivalent office in your country) provides important additional benefits, which we'll discuss in Chapter 2.

Duration of Copyright Protection

Copyright protection doesn't last forever, but it does last for a very long time. For works created by individual authors after January 1, 1978, copyright protection lasts for the life of the author plus 70 years.

For works created anonymously, pseudonymously, or as works made for hire, the copyright term is 95 years from publication or 120 years from creation, whichever is shorter. Different rules apply to works created before 1978, and copyright duration varies by country. However, for most self-publishers creating new works today, you can expect your copyright to protect your work throughout your lifetime and provide for your heirs for 70 years after your death.

After copyright expires, works enter the public domain, meaning anyone can use them without permission or payment.

The Difference Between Copyright, Trademark, and Patent

Authors sometimes confuse different types of intellectual property protection. Here's a quick overview of the main differences:

Copyright

- Protects original creative works (books, music, art, etc.)
- Protection is automatic upon creation
- Lasts for author's life plus 70 years (in most cases)
- Protects the expression of ideas, not the ideas themselves

Trademark

- Protects brand names, logos, slogans, and other identifiers
- Used to distinguish goods/services from others in the marketplace
- Can potentially last forever if properly maintained
- Relevant for authors when protecting series titles, pen names, or logos

Patent

- Protects inventions and discoveries
- Must be novel, non-obvious, and useful
- Requires formal application and examination process
- Lasts for 20 years from filing date
- Rarely relevant for authors unless their books describe patentable inventions

As an author, you'll primarily be concerned with copyright, though you might consider trademark protection for your brand elements if you develop a significant author platform or book series.

Copyright Ownership

By default, the creator of a work is the copyright owner. However, there are exceptions:

Works Made for Hire

If you hire someone to create content for your book (such as illustrations, cover design, or ghostwriting) under a "work made for hire" agreement, you—not the creator—own the copyright. This requires a written agreement specifically stating that the work is "made for hire."

Without such an agreement, you may only receive a license to use the work while the creator retains copyright ownership. This is why proper contracts are essential when working with designers, editors, and other professionals.

Joint Works

If you co-author a book, it becomes a "joint work," and each author owns an equal share of the copyright unless you agree otherwise in writing. Each co-author can exercise all copyright rights independently, subject to a duty to account to the other co-authors for any profits.

Transfer of Copyright

Copyright can be transferred to others through a written agreement. This is what happens in traditional publishing—authors typically transfer some or all of their copyright rights to the publisher through their publishing contract.

As a self-publisher on KDP, you retain your copyright while granting Amazon a non-exclusive license to distribute your work according to the KDP Terms of Service.

Copyright Notice

While not required for copyright protection, including a copyright notice in your book is still recommended. A proper copyright notice consists of:

1. The copyright symbol (©), the word "Copyright," or the abbreviation "Copr."
2. The year of first publication
3. The name of the copyright owner

Example: © 2025 Jane Smith

Including this notice informs readers that your work is protected and identifies you as the copyright owner. It also eliminates any potential "innocent infringement" defense, where someone claims they didn't know the work was protected.

We'll cover how to create a complete copyright page for your book in Chapter 3.

Summary

- Copyright automatically protects original works of authorship fixed in a tangible medium
- Copyright gives you exclusive rights to reproduce, distribute, display, perform, and create derivatives of your work
- Protection begins the moment you create your work; no registration or notice is required
- Copyright lasts for your lifetime plus 70 years (in most cases)
- Copyright protects the expression of ideas, not the ideas themselves
- You own the copyright to your work unless you've transferred it or created it as a work for hire

Understanding these fundamentals provides the foundation for making informed decisions about copyright registration, creating your copyright page, and protecting your rights as a self-published author—topics we'll explore in the following chapters.

Chapter 2: Copyright Registration

As we learned in Chapter 1, your work is automatically protected by copyright from the moment you create it. However, there's an important distinction between having automatic copyright protection and registering your copyright with the U.S. Copyright Office (or equivalent agency in your country). This chapter explores the benefits of registration, the registration process, and strategic considerations for when to register your work.

Automatic Copyright vs. Registration

Let's start by clarifying the difference between automatic copyright protection and formal registration:

Automatic Copyright Protection:

- Begins the moment your work is created and fixed in tangible form
- Requires no paperwork or filing
- Costs nothing
- Gives you the basic exclusive rights to your work

Copyright Registration:

- Requires filing an application with the Copyright Office

- Involves paying a registration fee

- Creates a public record of your copyright claim

- Provides additional legal benefits not available with automatic protection alone

While registration is not required for copyright protection to exist, it provides significant advantages that make it worth considering for serious self-published authors.

Benefits of Registering Your Copyright

Registering your copyright with the U.S. Copyright Office provides several important legal advantages:

1. Prerequisite for Infringement Lawsuits

For U.S. works, copyright registration is a prerequisite for filing an infringement lawsuit in federal court. Without registration, you cannot sue someone for infringing your copyright. This alone is a compelling reason to register works you believe have commercial value.

2. Statutory Damages and Attorney's Fees

If you register your copyright before an infringement occurs (or within three months of publication), you become eligible to seek statutory damages and attorney's fees in an infringement lawsuit.

Without registration, you can only recover actual damages (your financial losses) and the infringer's profits, which can be difficult and expensive to prove. Statutory damages, on the other hand, range from $750 to $30,000 per work infringed, and up to $150,000 per work for willful infringement—regardless of actual financial harm.

The ability to recover attorney's fees is also significant, as copyright litigation can be expensive. Without this provision, the cost of pursuing legal action might exceed the damages you could recover.

3. Prima Facie Evidence

Registration within five years of publication establishes prima facie evidence of the validity of your copyright and the facts stated in your certificate of registration. This means that in a legal proceeding, the court will presume these facts are true unless proven otherwise, shifting the burden of proof to the party challenging the copyright.

4. Public Record

Registration creates a public record of your copyright claim, making it easier for others to find you when they want to request permission to use your work. It also puts potential infringers on notice that your work is protected.

5. Customs Protection

Registration allows you to record your copyright with U.S. Customs and Border Protection to prevent the importation of infringing copies of your work.

How to Register Your Copyright

Registering your copyright with the U.S. Copyright Office is a straightforward process that can be completed online. Here's a step-by-step guide:

Step 1: Determine the Appropriate Registration Type

For most self-published books, you'll use one of these registration types:

- Literary Works: For most books, including fiction and non-fiction
- Visual Arts Works: If your book contains significant original artwork or illustrations
- Single Serial Issue: For periodicals, magazines, newsletters, etc.

Step 2: Create an Account on the Copyright Office Website

Visit the U.S. Copyright Office's Electronic Copyright Office (eCO) system and create an account if you don't already have one.

Step 3: Complete the Application

Log in to your account and select "Register a New Claim."
Follow the prompts to complete the application, which will ask
for information such as:

- Type of work you're registering
- Title of the work
- Author information (including pseudonyms if applicable)
- Year of completion
- Publication status and date (if published)
- Whether the work contains material previously
  registered or in the public domain
- The claimant (owner) of the copyright

Be accurate and thorough when completing this information,
as errors could affect the validity of your registration.

Step 4: Pay the Filing Fee

As of 2025, the standard filing fee for a single work by a single
author who is also the claimant is $45 when filed
electronically. Fees may be higher for other types of
registrations or paper filings. Check the Copyright Office's
current fee schedule for the most up-to-date information.

Step 5: Submit Your Deposit Copy

You must submit a copy of the work you're registering. For published books, this generally means uploading an electronic copy of your book in PDF format. For certain types of works or in specific circumstances, you may need to mail physical copies instead.

Follow the instructions provided during the application process regarding the appropriate deposit requirements for your specific work.

Step 6: Wait for Processing

After submitting your application, fee, and deposit, the Copyright Office will review your materials. This process can take several months (typically 3-9 months, though processing times vary). You can check the status of your application through your eCO account.

If there are no issues with your application, you'll eventually receive a certificate of registration by mail. If there are problems, the Copyright Office will contact you with questions or requests for additional information.

Registration Fees and Timeline

Current Registration Fees (as of 2025)

- $45: Single work by a single author who is also the claimant, filed electronically

- $65: All other online filings
- $125: Paper filings (using Form TX for literary works)
- $35: Single application (simplified application for single works by single authors)

These fees are subject to change, so always check the Copyright Office's current fee schedule before filing.

Processing Timeline

The Copyright Office's processing time varies depending on their workload and whether you file electronically or by paper. As of 2025:

- Electronic filings: Average 3-7 months
- Paper filings: Average 6-12 months

The effective date of registration is the date the Copyright Office receives all required elements (application, fee, and deposit) in acceptable form, regardless of how long processing takes.

When to Register: Before or After Publication?

One common question self-publishers face is whether to register their copyright before or after publishing their book. There are advantages and considerations for both approaches:

Registering Before Publication

Advantages:

- Establishes a clear record of your work before it enters the marketplace
- Ensures you're eligible for statutory damages and attorney's fees from day one
- Provides peace of mind that your work is fully protected before release

Considerations:

- If you make significant changes after registration but before publication, you might need to file for supplementary registration
- You'll need to pay the registration fee before knowing how well your book will sell

Registering After Publication

Advantages:

- You can register the final, published version of your work
- You can wait to see if your book gains traction before investing in registration
- You still have a three-month grace period after publication to register and maintain eligibility for statutory damages and attorney's fees

Considerations:

- If infringement occurs before registration, you lose the ability to claim statutory damages and attorney's fees
- The longer you wait, the more risk you take that someone might infringe your work before registration

Strategic Approach

A strategic approach many self-published authors take is:

1. For your first book or books you expect to be commercially significant: Register before publication or within three months of publication to ensure maximum protection.

2. For subsequent books in a series or books with less commercial potential: Consider waiting to see how they perform before registering, but be aware of the three-month window after publication if you want to maintain eligibility for statutory damages.

3. For books that achieve unexpected success: Register as soon as possible if you didn't register initially, even if it's beyond the three-month window. While you'll lose some benefits, registration is still valuable for establishing your rights and enabling you to file infringement lawsuits if needed.

Group Registration Options

If you're a prolific author publishing multiple works, the Copyright Office offers some cost-effective group registration options:

Group Registration of Short Online Literary Works (GRTX)

This option allows you to register up to 50 short online literary works (between 50 and 17,500 words) in a single application for a single fee. This is particularly useful for authors who publish short stories, essays, or articles online.

Group Registration of Unpublished Works (GRUW)

This option allows you to register up to 10 unpublished works by the same author(s) in a single application. This can be useful if you're preparing multiple books or stories that haven't been published yet.

Group Registration of Contributions to Periodicals (GRCP)

If you regularly contribute to magazines, newspapers, or other periodicals, this option allows you to register multiple contributions published within a 12-month period.

International Considerations

While this chapter focuses primarily on U.S. copyright registration, it's worth noting that copyright registration systems vary by country:

- Some countries, like Canada and the UK, have voluntary registration systems but don't require registration for full legal protection.
- Many countries don't have formal registration systems at all, as the Berne Convention (which we'll discuss in Chapter 4) prohibits requiring formalities as a condition of copyright protection.

If you plan to sell your books internationally (which is likely with KDP), understanding these differences becomes important. We'll explore international copyright considerations in more detail in Chapter 4.

Summary

- While copyright protection is automatic, registration provides significant additional benefits
- Registration is required before filing an infringement lawsuit in the U.S.
- Registering before infringement occurs (or within three months of publication) makes you eligible for statutory damages and attorney's fees

- The registration process involves completing an application, paying a fee, and submitting a copy of your work
- Consider registering works with commercial potential before publication or within three months of publication
- Group registration options can make protecting multiple works more cost-effective
- International copyright registration requirements vary by country

Understanding the benefits and process of copyright registration helps you make informed decisions about protecting your work. In the next chapter, we'll explore how to create an effective copyright page for your self-published book.

Chapter 3: Creating an Effective Copyright Page

The copyright page is often one of the most overlooked elements of a self-published book, yet it serves several important functions. It establishes your legal claim to your work, provides essential publication information, and can protect you from liability. In this chapter, we'll explore how to create an effective copyright page for your KDP book.

The Purpose of a Copyright Page

Before diving into the specifics, let's understand why the copyright page matters:

1. Legal protection: It formally declares your copyright ownership and warns against unauthorized reproduction.
2. Publication information: It provides essential details about the book, its publication, and the parties involved in its creation.
3. Professional appearance: A well-crafted copyright page gives your book a professional look that readers and industry professionals expect.
4. Liability protection: Disclaimers on the copyright page can help limit your legal liability, particularly for non-fiction works.
5. Cataloging information: It provides data that libraries and bookstores use to categorize your book.

While Amazon KDP doesn't require you to include a copyright page, doing so is strongly recommended for these reasons.

Essential Elements of a Copyright Page

A comprehensive copyright page typically includes several key elements. Not all are required, but together they create a thorough and professional presentation. Let's examine each element in detail:

1. Copyright Notice

The copyright notice is the most fundamental element of your copyright page. While not legally required for copyright protection (as we learned in Chapter 1), it serves as a clear statement of ownership and a deterrent against infringement. A standard copyright notice consists of three elements:

- The copyright symbol (©), the word "Copyright," or the abbreviation "Copr."
- The year of first publication
- The name of the copyright owner (usually the author or their company)

Example:

```
© 2025 Jane Smith
```

If you're using a pen name, you can either use that name in the copyright notice or use your legal name. If you've established a publishing company, you might use the company name instead:

© 2025 Midnight Press LLC

For updated editions, you might include multiple years:

© 2023, 2025 Jane Smith

This indicates the book was first published in 2023, with a new edition in 2025.

2. Rights Reserved Statement

Following the copyright notice, most books include a statement of rights reservation. The traditional phrase "All rights reserved" originated from the Buenos Aires Convention of 1910, which required this statement for copyright protection in certain countries.

While "All rights reserved" is no longer legally required in most countries, it's still commonly used and serves as a clear statement of intent. You can use the simple phrase or expand it for clarity:

Simple version:

Expanded version:

3. ISBN Information

If your book has an International Standard Book Number (ISBN), include it on the copyright page. Different formats (hardcover, paperback, ebook) should each have their own ISBN if applicable:

```
ISBN: 978-1-234567-89-0 (paperback)
ISBN: 978-1-234567-90-6 (ebook)
```

Note that if you use KDP's free ISBN option, Amazon is listed as the publisher of record. If you use your own ISBN (purchased from Bowker in the US or your country's ISBN agency), you or your publishing company will be listed as the publisher.

4. Publisher Information

Include the name of your publishing imprint or company and potentially contact information:

```
Published by Midnight Press LLC
www.midnightpressbooks.com
```

For self-publishers without a formal imprint, you might simply omit this or use your name.

5. Edition Information

If your book isn't a first edition, note which edition it is:

```
Second Edition: January 2025
```

You might also include printing information if relevant:

```
First Printing: January 2025
```

6. Disclaimers

Disclaimers are particularly important for non-fiction books to limit liability. The specific disclaimer depends on your book's content:

For a general non-fiction book:

> The information in this book is provided for informational purposes only and is not intended as professional advice. The author and publisher are not responsible for any damages resulting from the use of information contained in this book.

For a memoir or book based on real events:

> This is a work of memoir. While all events described are true to the author's recollection, some names, locations, and identifying characteristics have been changed to protect the privacy of individuals.

For a novel:

> This is a work of fiction. Names, characters, places, and incidents either are products of the author's imagination

or are used fictitiously. Any resemblance
to actual persons, living or dead,
events, or locales is entirely
coincidental.

For a health or medical book:

This book is not intended as a substitute
for the medical advice of physicians. The
reader should regularly consult a
physician in matters relating to their
health, particularly with respect to any
symptoms that may require diagnosis or
medical attention.

7. Credits

Acknowledge key contributors to your book, such as:

Cover design by John Designer
Interior formatting by Format
Professionals Inc.
Edited by Jane Editor

8. Permissions

If you've used copyrighted material with permission, acknowledge this:

```
Excerpt from "Famous Poem" by Famous Poet
used with permission of Famous Publishing
House.
```

9. Country of Printing

Some authors include where the book was printed:

```
Printed in the United States of America
```

For print-on-demand books through KDP, this information may vary depending on where the customer orders the book, so it's often omitted.

Sample Copyright Pages for Different Types of Books

Let's look at complete examples for different types of books:

Fiction Book Copyright Page

```
© 2025 Jane Smith


All rights reserved. No part of this
publication may be reproduced,
```

Published by Midnight Press LLC
www.midnightpressbooks.com

Cover design by John Designer
Edited by Jane Editor

ISBN: 978-1-234567-89-0 (paperback)

ISBN: 978-1-234567-90-6 (ebook)

First Edition: January 2025

Non-fiction Book Copyright Page

Published by Midnight Press LLC
www.midnightpressbooks.com

Cover design by John Designer

Interior formatting by Format Professionals Inc.

Edited by Jane Editor

ISBN: 978-1-234567-89-0 (paperback)

ISBN: 978-1-234567-90-6 (ebook)

First Edition: January 2025

Memoir Copyright Page

This is a work of memoir. While all
events described are true to the author's
recollection, some names, locations, and
identifying characteristics have been
changed to protect the privacy of
individuals.

Published by Midnight Press LLC
www.midnightpressbooks.com

Cover design by John Designer
Edited by Jane Editor

ISBN: 978-1-234567-89-0 (paperback)

ISBN: 978-1-234567-90-6 (ebook)

First Edition: January 2025

Public Domain Work with Original Content

If you're publishing a public domain work with your own original content (such as annotations, illustrations, or an introduction), you'll need to clarify what is and isn't protected by copyright:

Published by Midnight Press LLC

www.midnightpressbooks.com

Cover design and illustrations by John Designer

Introduction and annotations by Jane Smith

ISBN: 978-1-234567-89-0 (paperback)

ISBN: 978-1-234567-90-6 (ebook)

First Edition: January 2025

Placement and Formatting of the Copyright Page

The copyright page is traditionally placed on the verso (reverse side) of the title page, making it one of the first pages in your book. In ebooks, it typically appears after the title page and before the dedication or table of contents.

For formatting:

- Use a smaller font size than your main text (typically 9-10pt)
- Single spacing is standard
- Left alignment is most common, though some publishers center the text
- Keep the design simple and readable
- For print books, the copyright page is usually positioned at the bottom of the page rather than the top

Additional Elements to Consider

Depending on your book and publishing goals, you might consider adding these elements to your copyright page:

Library of Congress Control Number (LCCN)

If you've obtained an LCCN (useful if you want your book in libraries), include it:

```
Library of Congress Control Number:
2025901234
```

Cataloging-in-Publication (CIP) Data

Major publishers include CIP data, which helps libraries catalog books. As a self-publisher, you typically won't have access to this unless you pay a private service to create it.

Website or Contact Information

Including your author website or contact information can help readers connect with you:

```
For more information, visit:
www.janesmith.com
```

Trademark Notices

If your book contains trademarked terms, you might include notices:

```
BRAND NAME® is a registered trademark of
Brand Company, Inc.
```

Common Copyright Page Mistakes to Avoid

When creating your copyright page, avoid these common mistakes:

1. Omitting the copyright page entirely: Even a basic copyright notice is better than none.
2. Using outdated or incorrect language: Research current copyright conventions rather than copying from old books.

3. Claiming rights you don't have: Don't claim copyright on public domain works or content you don't own.

4. Including unnecessary information: Keep your copyright page focused and professional.

5. Poor formatting: A messy copyright page suggests amateur publishing.

6. Inappropriate disclaimers: Ensure your disclaimers are relevant to your specific book.

7. Missing ISBN information: If you have ISBNs, include them correctly.

Copyright Page for Digital vs. Print Books

While the core elements remain the same, there are some differences to consider when creating copyright pages for different formats:

Print Books

- Include all relevant ISBNs
- May include printing location and edition information
- Typically positioned at the bottom of the verso page

Ebooks

- Include the ebook ISBN if you have one

- May include links to your website or social media (make them clickable)

  Consider adding language about digital rights:

-

Summary

A well-crafted copyright page serves multiple purposes: it establishes your legal claim to your work, provides essential information about your book, and presents a professional appearance to readers and industry professionals. While not all elements are required, including the core components—copyright notice, rights reserved statement, and relevant disclaimers—helps protect your work and demonstrates your professionalism as an author.

Remember that the copyright page is often the first impression readers get of your book's interior, so taking the time to create a proper copyright page is worth the effort. Use the templates provided in this chapter as starting points, and customize them to fit your specific book and publishing needs.

In the next chapter, we'll explore international copyright considerations, which are particularly important for KDP authors whose books are available in global markets.

Chapter 4: International Copyright Considerations

As a self-published author on KDP, your books can reach readers worldwide with just a few clicks. While this global reach creates tremendous opportunities, it also introduces complex international copyright considerations. This chapter explores how copyright works across borders, the key international agreements that protect your work, and strategies for managing your rights in the global marketplace.

The Global Nature of KDP Publishing

When you publish through Amazon KDP, your book becomes available in multiple Amazon marketplaces around the world, including:

- United States (amazon.com)

- United Kingdom (amazon.co.uk)

- Germany (amazon.de)

- France (amazon.fr)

- Spain (amazon.es)

- Italy (amazon.it)

- Netherlands (amazon.nl)

- Japan (amazon.co.jp)

- Brazil (amazon.com.br)

- Canada (amazon.ca)

- Australia (amazon.com.au)

- India (amazon.in)

- Mexico (amazon.com.mx)

This global distribution means your work is subject to the copyright laws of multiple countries simultaneously. Understanding how these laws interact is essential for protecting your rights internationally.

The Berne Convention and International Copyright Protection

The foundation of international copyright protection is the Berne Convention for the Protection of Literary and Artistic Works, first established in 1886 and subsequently revised several times. As of 2025, the Berne Convention has over 180 member countries, making it the most significant international copyright agreement.

Key Principles of the Berne Convention

1. National Treatment: Member countries must give authors from other member countries the same copyright protection they give to their own citizens. This means your book receives the same protection in Germany or Japan as works by German or Japanese authors.

2. Automatic Protection: Copyright protection is automatic upon creation of the work; no registration or other formalities are required. This principle ensures your work is protected internationally even if you haven't registered it in each country.

3. Independence of Protection: Protection in the country of origin is independent of protection in other countries. This means that even if copyright expires in one country, it may still be protected in others.

4. Minimum Standards: The Convention establishes minimum standards of protection that all member countries must provide, including:

- Protection for the author's lifetime plus at least 50 years (though many countries extend this to 70 years)
- Exclusive rights to reproduce, translate, adapt, perform, and broadcast the work
- Moral rights (the right to claim authorship and object to modifications that would harm the author's reputation)

What This Means for KDP Authors

Thanks to the Berne Convention, when you publish your book on KDP:

- Your work is automatically protected by copyright in all Berne Convention member countries
- You don't need to register your copyright in each country (though registration in your home country still provides benefits, as discussed in Chapter 2)
- You can enforce your rights in foreign countries according to their local laws

Other Important International Copyright Treaties

While the Berne Convention forms the foundation of international copyright protection, several other agreements further strengthen and harmonize copyright laws globally:

Universal Copyright Convention (UCC)

Established in 1952 and administered by UNESCO, the UCC was created as an alternative to the Berne Convention with less stringent requirements. Since most countries are now Berne members, the UCC has become less significant, but it still provides a bridge between Berne and non-Berne countries.

WIPO Copyright Treaty (WCT)

Adopted in 1996, the WCT extends copyright protection to computer programs and databases and addresses digital technologies. It requires member countries to provide legal remedies against the circumvention of technological measures used to protect copyrighted works (like DRM on ebooks).

Agreement on Trade-Related Aspects of Intellectual Property Rights (TRIPS)

Part of the World Trade Organization (WTO) framework, TRIPS establishes minimum standards for intellectual property protection and enforcement among WTO members. It incorporates the substantive provisions of the Berne

Convention and adds enforcement mechanisms through trade sanctions.

The Marrakesh Treaty

Adopted in 2013, this treaty facilitates access to published works for people who are blind, visually impaired, or otherwise print disabled. It creates limitations and exceptions to copyright to allow the creation and distribution of accessible format copies.

Copyright Duration in Different Countries

One of the most significant variations in international copyright law is the duration of protection. While the Berne Convention establishes a minimum standard of the author's life plus 50 years, many countries have extended this period:

- Life + 70 years: United States, European Union countries, United Kingdom, Australia, Brazil, Russia
- Life + 75 years: Guatemala, Honduras
- Life + 80 years: Colombia, Mexico
- Life + 100 years: Mexico (for some works created before 1928)

A few countries still maintain the Berne minimum of life + 50 years, including Canada, Japan, New Zealand, and China.

This variation means your work may enter the public domain at different times in different countries. For example, a book by an author who died in 1955 would be in the public domain in Canada as of 2006 but would remain protected in the United States until 2026.

The "Rule of the Shorter Term"

Many countries apply what's known as the "rule of the shorter term," which means they will not protect a foreign work for longer than it would be protected in its country of origin. This principle, allowed under the Berne Convention, can further complicate the international copyright landscape.

For example, if you're a Canadian author (where copyright lasts for life + 50 years), your work might receive only 50 years of protection after your death in countries like France or Germany, even though their domestic works receive 70 years of protection.

Copyright Registration Around the World

As we discussed in Chapter 2, copyright registration in the United States provides significant legal advantages, even though protection is automatic. The approach to registration varies widely in other countries:

- United States: Registration is not required for protection but is necessary for filing an infringement lawsuit and obtaining statutory damages.
- United Kingdom, Canada, Australia: No formal registration system; copyright is entirely automatic with no registration option or requirement.
- Germany, France: No registration system; instead, authors may deposit copies with national libraries for evidentiary purposes.
- Spain, Mexico: Voluntary registration systems exist but are not required for protection.
- China: Voluntary registration system that provides strong evidentiary value in enforcement actions.
- Japan: Voluntary registration system primarily for recording transfers of rights.

If your book achieves significant success in a particular foreign market, you might consider investigating the local registration or deposit options in that country, particularly in places like China where enforcement can be challenging without local registration.

International Enforcement Challenges

While your work is theoretically protected worldwide, enforcing your rights internationally presents practical challenges:

Jurisdictional Issues

Copyright infringement lawsuits typically must be filed in the country where the infringement occurred. This means you might need to engage legal counsel in multiple countries to address widespread infringement.

Cost and Complexity

International litigation is expensive and complex, often requiring specialized attorneys familiar with both copyright law and international legal procedures.

Varying Standards

Different countries have different standards for what constitutes infringement, fair use/fair dealing, and available remedies.

Online Infringement

Digital piracy often crosses multiple jurisdictions, making enforcement particularly challenging. A pirate website might be hosted in one country, operated from another, and accessible worldwide.

Practical Strategies for International Copyright Management

Given these complexities, here are practical strategies for KDP authors to manage their international copyright effectively:

1. Focus on Prevention

- Use digital rights management (DRM) for your ebooks if you're concerned about piracy (though opinions on DRM effectiveness vary)
- Include clear copyright notices in all editions
- Consider watermarking digital review copies
- Monitor the internet for unauthorized copies using tools like Google Alerts or specialized services

2. Prioritize Major Markets

Rather than trying to enforce your rights everywhere, focus on your largest markets where infringement has the most significant impact on your sales.

3. Use Amazon's Infringement Reporting Tools

Amazon provides mechanisms to report copyright infringement on their platforms worldwide. If you find unauthorized copies of your book on any Amazon marketplace, report them through Amazon's infringement reporting process.

4. Consider International Rights Management

If your book gains significant traction, consider working with a literary agent or rights manager who specializes in international rights to help navigate foreign markets and protect your work abroad.

5. Understand International Licensing

When licensing rights to foreign publishers (for translations, for example), ensure your contracts clearly specify:

- The territories covered
- The languages included
- The formats permitted (print, ebook, audiobook)
- The duration of the license
- Royalty rates and payment terms
- Reversion clauses if the book goes out of print

Translation Rights and Foreign Editions

One of the most valuable international rights for successful books is translation rights. As a self-published author, you retain these rights unless you explicitly license them to someone else.

Options for Translations

1. License to a foreign publisher: The traditional approach is to license translation rights to a publisher in the target country who handles translation, production, and distribution.
2. Commission your own translations: Some successful KDP authors hire translators directly and publish translated editions through KDP.
3. Amazon Translation Services: Amazon occasionally offers translation services to select KDP authors for promising titles, though this is by invitation only.

If you pursue option 1, be aware that standard translation rights deals typically offer:

- An advance against royalties (the amount varies widely by market and genre)
- Royalty rates of 6-10% of retail price or 20-30% of net receipts
- Term limits of 5-7 years, after which rights can revert if certain conditions are met

Public Domain Variations by Country

If you're publishing works based on public domain material, be aware that a work might be in the public domain in one country but still protected in another due to different copyright terms.

For example, works by authors who died before 1955 are in the public domain in Canada but may still be protected in the United States and European Union. This can affect your ability to distribute derivative works or translations in certain countries.

International Implications of Amazon's KDP Select Program

If you enroll your book in KDP Select, you grant Amazon exclusive distribution rights for the ebook format worldwide for 90-day periods. This means you cannot sell your ebook through other retailers in any country during this period, though print and audiobook versions can still be distributed elsewhere.

Consider this global exclusivity carefully, especially if you have strong sales potential in markets where Amazon isn't dominant. For example, in some European countries, local ebook platforms may have significant market share that you'd be unable to access while in KDP Select.

Summary

Publishing through KDP makes you a global author, with your work protected by a patchwork of international copyright laws and treaties. The Berne Convention provides a foundation of automatic protection across most countries, but significant variations exist in duration, registration systems, and enforcement mechanisms.

While international copyright enforcement presents challenges, focusing on prevention, prioritizing major markets, and leveraging Amazon's global infrastructure can help protect your work worldwide. As your career grows, understanding international rights management becomes increasingly important, particularly regarding translations and foreign editions.

In the next chapter, we'll explore how to legally use others' work in your book, including fair use principles, obtaining permissions, and working with public domain materials.

Chapter 5: Using Others' Work in Your Book

As an author, you may want to incorporate others' creative works into your book—whether it's quoting a poem, including song lyrics, reproducing images, or referencing another author's ideas. Understanding when and how you can legally use others' work is crucial to avoid copyright infringement. This chapter explores the legal frameworks that govern using copyrighted material, with a focus on fair use, obtaining permissions, public domain works, and proper citation.

Fair Use Doctrine and Its Limitations

The fair use doctrine is perhaps the most important—and most misunderstood—concept in copyright law for authors. It allows limited use of copyrighted material without permission for purposes such as criticism, comment, news reporting, teaching, scholarship, or research.

The Four Factors of Fair Use

Courts evaluate fair use claims based on four factors:

1. The purpose and character of the use
   - Is your use commercial or non-commercial?
   - Is your use transformative (adding new meaning, message, or purpose)?
   - Educational and critical uses generally favor fair use.
2. The nature of the copyrighted work
   - Using factual works is more likely to be fair use than using highly creative works.

- Published works are easier to claim fair use for than unpublished works.
3. The amount and substantiality of the portion used
   - Using small portions favors fair use.
   - Even small portions may not be fair use if they constitute the "heart" of the work.
4. The effect on the potential market for the original work
   - If your use negatively impacts the market for the original work, it's less likely to be fair use.
   - This is often considered the most important factor.

Common Fair Use Misconceptions

Many self-published authors operate under misconceptions about fair use:

Misconception #1: "If I only use X words, it's automatically fair use."

Reality: There is no specific word count or percentage that automatically qualifies as fair use. Courts evaluate all four factors together.

Misconception #2: "If I give credit to the author, it's fair use."

Reality: Attribution is important but doesn't transform an infringing use into a fair use. You can properly cite a source and still infringe copyright.

> Misconception #3: "If I'm not making money from my book, it's fair use."

Reality: While commercial use weighs against fair use, non-commercial use doesn't automatically make something fair use. All four factors are considered.

> Misconception #4: "If I change it a little bit, it's fair use."

Reality: Minor changes don't necessarily create a transformative work. Substantial transformation that adds new meaning or message is required.

Fair Use Examples for Authors

To illustrate how fair use might apply in practice, consider these examples:

Likely Fair Use:

- Quoting a few lines from a book in a literary analysis or review
- Including a small portion of a song lyric that you then analyze critically
- Using a short excerpt from a historical document in a historical novel for authenticity

- Reproducing a small portion of a chart or graph in a non-fiction book that analyzes the data

Likely Not Fair Use:

- Including multiple stanzas of a poem purely for aesthetic purposes
- Reproducing entire song lyrics as chapter epigraphs without analysis
- Using substantial portions of another author's work without adding significant commentary
- Including others' photographs or artwork as illustrations without permission

The Risk Assessment Approach

Because fair use is determined case-by-case and can be unpredictable, many publishers and authors take a risk assessment approach:

1. Evaluate the four factors honestly for your specific use case.
2. Consider the litigation risk (how likely is the copyright owner to discover and object to your use?).
3. Assess the potential damages if your fair use claim fails.
4. Decide whether to: use the material under fair use, seek permission, or find alternative content.

For self-published authors, the safest approach is often to seek permission when in doubt, especially for uses that are commercial in nature or use substantial portions of creative works.

Obtaining Permissions

When your use of copyrighted material doesn't qualify as fair use, you'll need to obtain permission from the copyright holder.

Identifying the Copyright Holder

The first step is identifying who owns the copyright, which isn't always straightforward:

- For books: Start with the publisher, but be aware that rights may have reverted to the author or their estate.
- For songs: Typically, music publishers control the rights to lyrics and composition, while record labels control sound recordings.
- For images: The photographer or artist usually owns the copyright, but they may have transferred rights to an agency or publisher.
- For articles: The publication or the individual journalist might own the rights, depending on their contract.

Resources for finding copyright holders include:

- The U.S. Copyright Office's online records (for registered works)
- The publisher's permissions department
- Literary agencies representing the author
- Organizations like ASCAP, BMI, or SESAC for music
- Stock photo agencies for images

The Permission Request Process

Once you've identified the copyright holder, follow these steps:

1. Prepare a clear permission request that includes:
   - Specific details about the material you want to use
   - How you plan to use it (context, amount, format)
   - The nature of your publication (title, publisher, price, print run or distribution)
   - Your timeline
2. Send the request to the appropriate permissions department or individual.
3. Be prepared to negotiate terms, which may include:
   - A one-time fee
   - Royalty payments
   - Specific attribution requirements
   - Limitations on formats, territories, or duration

4. Get the permission in writing and keep records of all correspondence.

5. Follow all requirements in the permission agreement, including proper attribution.

Sample Permission Request Letter

[Your Name]

[Your Address]

[Your Email and Phone]

[Date]

[Rights Holder Name]

[Rights Holder Address]

Re: Permission Request for [Work Title]

Dear [Rights Holder],

I am writing to request permission to include [specific description of the material] from [title of work] by [author/creator] in my forthcoming book [your book title].

My book is [brief description of your book] and will be self-published through Amazon's Kindle Direct Publishing platform. I anticipate publishing in [month/year] with an estimated initial distribution of [number] copies in both print and ebook formats, priced at approximately [price range].

I would like to use [describe exactly what you want to use, including page numbers, word count, or other specific identifiers]. The material would be used [explain context - e.g., "as an epigraph for Chapter 3" or "as part of a critical analysis of contemporary poetry"].

Full credit will be given to the author and publisher as you specify. If you are not the rights holder for this material, I would appreciate it if you could direct me to the appropriate person or entity.

Thank you for considering this request. I look forward to your response.

Sincerely,
[Your Name]

Common Permission Fees

Permission fees vary widely depending on the material, usage, and rights holder. As a general guideline:

- Text excerpts: $50-$500 for small portions
- Song lyrics: $150-$1,000+ per song (even for short excerpts)
- Images: $25-$300+ depending on placement, size, and prominence
- Academic journal articles: $100-$500 for excerpts

Many rights holders have standard fee structures, while others evaluate requests case by case. Some may waive fees for academic or limited-distribution works.

When Permission Is Denied or Too Expensive

If permission is denied or the fee is beyond your budget, you have several options:

1. Revise your work to remove the copyrighted material.

2. Paraphrase the content instead of quoting directly (facts and ideas aren't copyrightable, only their expression).
3. Find alternative material that serves a similar purpose.
4. Create your own original content to replace the material.
5. Look for similar material in the public domain.

Public Domain Works

Works in the public domain are free for anyone to use without permission or payment. Understanding what is and isn't in the public domain can save you time and money.

What Is in the Public Domain

In the United States, public domain works include:

1. Works with expired copyright protection:
   - Works published in the U.S. before 1928 (as of 2025)
   - Works published between 1928 and 1963 whose copyright was not renewed
   - Works published without a copyright notice before 1989
2. Works created by the U.S. federal government:
   - Federal laws, regulations, and court decisions

- Federal government reports, studies, and publications
- Note: This applies only to federal government works, not state or local government works, which may be protected

3. Works explicitly dedicated to the public domain by their creators

Determining Public Domain Status

Determining whether a work is in the public domain can be complex:

1. For works published before 1928: These are definitely in the public domain in the U.S.

2. For works published between 1928 and 1963: Check the U.S. Copyright Office records for renewal information. If copyright wasn't renewed, the work is in the public domain.

3. For works published between 1964 and 1977: These works received automatic renewal and are still protected if they were published with a copyright notice.

4. For works published after 1977: These are almost certainly still protected by copyright.

5. For unpublished works: Copyright generally lasts for the life of the author plus 70 years.

Remember that public domain status varies by country, as discussed in Chapter 4. A work may be in the public domain in one country but protected in another.

Public Domain Resources

Several resources can help you find public domain works:

- Project Gutenberg (gutenberg.org): Over 60,000 free ebooks
- Wikimedia Commons (commons.wikimedia.org): Images, audio, and video files
- LibriVox (librivox.org): Public domain audiobooks
- USA.gov: U.S. government publications
- Creative Commons Search (search.creativecommons.org): Helps find content you can use, including public domain works

Using Public Domain Works

When using public domain works, keep these points in mind:

1. Verify the public domain status carefully before use.
2. Be aware that new elements added to public domain works may be protected. For example, a new translation of a public domain novel may have its own copyright.
3. Consider indicating the public domain status in your attribution to inform readers.

4. Remember that while the original work is free to use, your specific arrangement, selection, or presentation of public domain materials may be eligible for copyright protection as a derivative work.

Creative Commons Licenses

Creative Commons (CC) licenses provide a middle ground between "all rights reserved" copyright and the public domain. They allow creators to specify which rights they reserve and which they waive, making it easier for others to use their work under certain conditions.

Types of Creative Commons Licenses

Creative Commons offers six main license types, from most to least permissive:

1. CC BY (Attribution): You can use the work for any purpose, including commercially, as long as you give credit to the creator.
2. CC BY-SA (Attribution-ShareAlike): You can use and adapt the work, even commercially, but you must credit the creator and license your new creation under identical terms.

3. CC BY-ND (Attribution-NoDerivatives): You can use the work, even commercially, but you cannot create derivatives, and you must credit the creator.

4. CC BY-NC (Attribution-NonCommercial): You can use and adapt the work, but only for non-commercial purposes, and you must credit the creator.

5. CC BY-NC-SA (Attribution-NonCommercial-ShareAlike): You can use and adapt the work for non-commercial purposes, but you must credit the creator and license your new creation under identical terms.

6. CC BY-NC-ND (Attribution-NonCommercial-NoDerivatives): The most restrictive license; you can download and share the work with credit, but you cannot change it or use it commercially.

Using CC-Licensed Works in Your Book

When using Creative Commons licensed works:

1. Check if your use complies with the license terms. For commercial books, you can only use works with licenses that allow commercial use (CC BY, CC BY-SA, or CC BY-ND).

2. Provide proper attribution as specified by the license, typically including:
   - Title of the work

- Name of the creator
- Source URL
- License type with link to license

3. Be aware of the ShareAlike requirement if present, which may require you to license your entire book under the same CC license—a significant consideration for commercial authors.
4. Keep records of where you found the work and which license applied at the time of use.

Citing Sources Properly

Proper citation serves both ethical and legal purposes. It gives credit to original creators, helps readers find your sources, and can help strengthen fair use claims.

Citation Basics for Different Types of Works

While citation styles vary (APA, MLA, Chicago, etc.), basic elements include:

For Books:

- Author's name
- Title of the book
- Publisher
- Year of publication
- Page number(s) for specific quotes

For Articles:

- Author's name
- Title of the article
- Publication name
- Date of publication
- Page number(s) or URL

For Websites:

- Author's name (if available)
- Title of the page or article
- Website name
- URL
- Date accessed

For Images:

- Creator's name
- Title of the image
- Source/website
- Date created (if available)
- License information

Citation vs. Permission

Remember that citation alone doesn't replace the need for permission when using copyrighted material beyond fair use. Proper citation is necessary but not sufficient for copyright compliance.

Plagiarism vs. Copyright Infringement

It's important to understand the distinction:

- Plagiarism is an ethical issue involving passing off someone else's work or ideas as your own. It can occur even with public domain works.
- Copyright infringement is a legal issue involving using protected works without permission or a valid exception like fair use.

You can avoid plagiarism through proper citation but still commit copyright infringement if you use substantial portions without permission. Conversely, you can get permission and avoid copyright infringement but still commit plagiarism if you fail to acknowledge your sources.

Special Considerations for Different Types of Content

Quotes and Text Excerpts

- Brief quotes for criticism or review purposes generally fall under fair use.
- Longer excerpts or quotes used for aesthetic purposes typically require permission.
- Academic and scholarly works have more leeway under fair use than commercial fiction.

Song Lyrics and Poetry

- Even short excerpts of song lyrics and poetry typically require permission.
- Music publishers and poetry rights holders are known to actively protect their rights.
- Fees for song lyrics can be substantial, often $150-$500 for just a few lines.

Images and Artwork

- Using others' images almost always requires permission unless they're in the public domain or under a suitable Creative Commons license.
- Consider commissioning original artwork or using stock photos with appropriate licenses.
- Remember that finding an image through Google doesn't make it free to use.

Facts, Data, and Ideas

- Facts and ideas themselves are not copyrightable, only their specific expression.
- You can freely use factual information as long as you express it in your own words.
- Data compilations may have thin copyright protection for their selection and arrangement.

Titles and Short Phrases

- Titles, names, and short phrases are generally not protected by copyright.
- However, they might be protected by trademark law if they're used to identify a brand or product.
- You can typically use another book's title in your work without copyright concerns.

Practical Workflow for Using Others' Content

Follow this workflow when considering using others' content in your book:

1. Identify the material you want to use and its copyright status.
2. Evaluate whether your use qualifies as fair use by analyzing the four factors honestly.
3. If not fair use, identify the rights holder and request permission.
4. If permission is granted, follow all requirements for attribution and payment.
5. If permission is denied or too expensive, consider alternatives:
   - Use public domain or Creative Commons content

- Create original content
- Paraphrase or summarize instead of quoting
- Reduce the amount used to strengthen a fair use claim

6. Document everything: Keep records of your fair use analysis, permission requests, granted permissions, and sources of public domain or Creative Commons content.

Summary

Using others' work in your book requires careful navigation of copyright law. While fair use provides some flexibility, it has significant limitations, particularly for commercial works. When in doubt, seeking permission is the safest approach, though it may involve fees and negotiations.

Public domain works and Creative Commons licensed content offer valuable alternatives that can be used with fewer restrictions, provided you verify their status and comply with any license terms. Regardless of copyright status, proper citation is an ethical requirement that helps readers locate your sources and strengthens your credibility as an author.

By understanding these principles and following a systematic approach to using others' content, you can enhance your book while respecting intellectual property rights and minimizing legal risks.

In the next chapter, we'll explore strategies for protecting your own work from infringement, including monitoring for unauthorized use and taking action when your rights are violated.

Chapter 6: Protecting Your Work from Infringement

As a self-published author, you've invested significant time, creativity, and resources into creating your book. Protecting this investment from unauthorized use is an important aspect of managing your intellectual property. This chapter explores practical strategies for monitoring for infringement, responding to unauthorized use, and leveraging legal tools to protect your work in the digital age.

Understanding Copyright Infringement

Before diving into protection strategies, it's important to understand what constitutes copyright infringement. Copyright infringement occurs when someone uses your copyrighted work without permission in a way that violates one or more of your exclusive rights, such as:

- Reproducing your work (making copies)
- Creating derivative works based on your original
- Distributing copies of your work
- Publicly displaying or performing your work

Not all unauthorized uses constitute infringement. As we discussed in Chapter 5, fair use and other exceptions may apply. Additionally, you can only claim infringement for the original, creative elements of your work—not for facts, ideas, or common elements.

Common Types of Infringement for Self-Published Authors

Self-published authors typically encounter several forms of infringement:

1. Digital Piracy

Digital piracy involves unauthorized reproduction and distribution of your ebook through:

- Pirate websites offering free downloads
- File-sharing networks
- Social media groups sharing unauthorized copies

- Unauthorized sales on legitimate platforms by third parties

2. Counterfeit Print Books

Physical counterfeiting includes:

- Unauthorized printed copies sold online or in person
- Print-on-demand services used to create unauthorized copies
- Bound photocopies sold as originals

3. Plagiarism and Content Scraping

This involves others incorporating substantial portions of your work into their own:

- Text copied directly into another book
- Blog posts or articles reproducing your content
- "Spinners" who slightly modify your text to avoid detection

4. Unauthorized Translations

Without permission, others may:

- Translate your work into other languages
- Publish and sell these translations
- Distribute free translated versions online

5. Derivative Works

These include unauthorized:

- Adaptations of your work into different formats
- Sequels or prequels based on your characters and world
- Audiobook versions created without permission

Monitoring for Unauthorized Use

The first step in protecting your work is knowing when infringement occurs. Here are effective monitoring strategies:

1. Set Up Google Alerts

Google Alerts (alerts.google.com) is a free service that notifies you when new content matching your specified terms appears online:

- Set up alerts for your book title (in quotation marks for exact matches)
- Include your author name in alerts
- Create alerts for distinctive phrases from your book
- Set alerts for character names if they're unique

Example alert queries:

- "The Midnight Chronicles" John Smith
- "John Smith author"
- "distinctive unique phrase from your book"

2. Regular Search Engine Checks

Supplement automated alerts with manual searches:

- Use different search engines (Google, Bing, DuckDuckGo)
- Search for your book title plus terms like "PDF," "free download," or "epub"
- Use image search to find your book cover being used elsewhere
- Search international sites if your book is available globally

3. Monitor Online Marketplaces

Regularly check major online retailers:

- Amazon (including international marketplaces)
- eBay
- Etsy
- AliExpress
- Facebook Marketplace

Look for unauthorized copies, suspiciously low-priced versions, or listings using your cover image.

4. Use Specialized Anti-Piracy Tools

Several services specifically monitor for book piracy:

- Blasty (monitors and sends takedown notices)
- Muso (digital content protection service)
- Digimarc (digital watermarking and monitoring)
- AuthorPatrol (specialized book piracy monitoring)

These services typically charge monthly or annual fees, so evaluate their cost against your book's sales and piracy risk.

5. Join Author Communities

Author communities often share information about piracy sites and infringement:

- Facebook groups for authors in your genre
- Forums like KBoards or the KDP Community
- Professional organizations like the Authors Guild

Members frequently alert each other when they discover piracy sites targeting multiple authors.

DMCA Takedown Notices

The Digital Millennium Copyright Act (DMCA) provides a powerful tool for removing infringing content from websites and online platforms. Understanding how to use DMCA takedown notices effectively is essential for self-published authors.

What Is a DMCA Takedown Notice?

A DMCA takedown notice is a formal request to a website, hosting provider, or online platform to remove content that infringes your copyright. Under the DMCA, service providers must respond to properly formatted notices to maintain their "safe harbor" protection from liability.

Elements of an Effective DMCA Takedown Notice

A proper DMCA takedown notice must include:

1. Your contact information (name, address, phone number, email)
2. Identification of your copyrighted work that has been infringed
3. Identification of the infringing material and its location (specific URLs)
4. A statement of "good faith belief" that the use is not authorized
5. A statement of accuracy and "under penalty of perjury" that you are the copyright owner or authorized to act on their behalf
6. Your physical or electronic signature

Sample DMCA Takedown Notice Template

```
[Your Name]
[Your Address]
[Your Email]
[Your Phone Number]
[Date]


DMCA Copyright Infringement Notification
```

To Whom It May Concern:

I, [Your Name], am the copyright owner of [Book Title]. It has come to my attention that your website/service is hosting/distributing unauthorized copies of my copyrighted work at the following location(s):

[List specific URLs where the infringing content appears]

The original copyrighted work is available at:
[URL to your book on Amazon or other official retailers]

I have a good faith belief that the use of the described material in the manner complained of is not authorized by me, the copyright owner, or the law.

I swear, under penalty of perjury, that the information in this notification is accurate and that I am the copyright owner or am authorized to act on behalf of the owner of an exclusive right that is allegedly infringed.

I request that you immediately remove or disable access to this material.

Sincerely,

[Your Signature]

[Your Name]

Where to Send DMCA Notices

Send your DMCA notice to:

1. The website hosting the infringing content: Look for "DMCA," "Copyright," or "Legal" links, usually in the footer of the website.
2. The hosting provider: If the website doesn't respond, you can escalate to their hosting provider. Use WHOIS lookup tools (like whois.domaintools.com) to identify the host.

3. Search engines: Submit DMCA notices to Google and other search engines to remove infringing links from search results:
   - Google: https://support.google.com/legal/answer/3110420
   - Bing: https://www.microsoft.com/info/FormForDMCA.aspx
4. Online marketplaces and platforms: Major platforms have specific DMCA procedures:
   - Amazon: https://www.amazon.com/report/infringement
   - eBay: https://www.ebay.com/help/policies/listing-policies/selling-policies/intellectual-property-vero-program?id=4349
   - Facebook: https://www.facebook.com/help/contact/634636770043106

Tips for Effective DMCA Notices

1. Be specific and accurate: Provide exact URLs, not just website names.

2. Document everything: Keep copies of all notices sent and responses received.
3. Follow up: If you don't receive a response within 1-2 weeks, send a follow-up.
4. Be prepared for counter-notices: The alleged infringer may file a counter-notice claiming their use is legitimate. If this happens, you'll need to decide whether to pursue legal action.
5. Consider professional help: For widespread infringement, consider using a DMCA service or consulting an attorney.

Dealing with Piracy

Book piracy is a common concern for self-published authors. Here's a strategic approach to addressing it:

Assess the Impact

Not all piracy is equally harmful:

- High-impact piracy: Counterfeit copies sold on legitimate platforms directly competing with your book
- Medium-impact piracy: Easily accessible free downloads on prominent websites
- Low-impact piracy: Obscure websites with limited traffic or poor-quality copies

Focus your enforcement efforts on high-impact cases that genuinely affect your sales.

Prioritize Your Response

Given limited time and resources, prioritize your anti-piracy efforts:

1. First priority: Counterfeit copies on major retailers (Amazon, Barnes & Noble)
2. Second priority: High-traffic piracy sites ranking well in search results
3. Third priority: Social media groups or forums sharing your work
4. Lower priority: Small, obscure sites with limited visibility

Prevention Strategies

Several approaches can help reduce piracy:

1. Digital watermarking: Include invisible identifiers in your ebooks that can trace leaked copies back to their source.
2. Use DRM selectively: Digital Rights Management can deter casual copying, though it's controversial and can frustrate legitimate readers. Consider the trade-offs for your specific situation.
3. Include a copyright notice and personal appeal: A friendly note asking readers to respect your work and

explaining how piracy impacts you can discourage some sharing.

4. Release free content legitimately: Offering some content for free (like the first book in a series) can reduce the incentive for piracy while building your audience.

5. Competitive pricing: Reasonably priced books reduce the motivation for seeking pirated copies.

The Whack-a-Mole Problem

Be aware that fighting piracy can sometimes feel like playing whack-a-mole—when one site is taken down, others may appear. Consider these approaches:

1. Focus on containment rather than elimination: You may not eliminate all piracy, but you can reduce its visibility and impact.

2. Target the most harmful instances: Prioritize cases where someone is profiting from your work or significantly impacting your sales.

3. Consider the Streisand effect: Sometimes, drawing attention to piracy can inadvertently increase it. Address issues quietly when possible.

4. Evaluate ROI: Balance the time and resources spent fighting piracy against potential recovered sales.

When to Involve Legal Counsel

While many copyright issues can be handled independently, some situations warrant professional legal assistance:

Scenarios That May Require an Attorney

1. Commercial infringement: Someone is selling unauthorized copies or derivatives of your work and generating significant revenue.

2. Persistent infringement: A party continues infringing after multiple takedown notices.

3. Counter-notices: You receive a counter-notice challenging your DMCA takedown.

4. Complex international issues: Infringement occurs in countries with different copyright laws.

5. Substantial damages: The infringement has caused significant financial harm.

6. Registration issues: You need to expedite copyright registration to pursue an infringement case.

Finding the Right Attorney

When seeking legal counsel:

1. Look for intellectual property specialists: General practice attorneys may not have the specialized knowledge needed.

2. Consider experience with authors: Attorneys familiar with publishing understand the industry's unique aspects.

3. Ask about fee structures: Some attorneys offer contingency arrangements or flat fees for specific services.

4. Explore professional organizations: The Authors Guild and similar organizations often provide legal resources or referrals.

Cost-Benefit Analysis

Before pursuing legal action, carefully consider:

1. Potential recovery: What damages might you realistically recover?

2. Legal costs: Attorney fees, court costs, and time investment

3. Likelihood of success: How strong is your case?

4. Collectability: Even if you win, can the infringer pay damages?

5. Alternative resolutions: Could a cease-and-desist letter or negotiated settlement work?

Amazon's Copyright Infringement Policies

As a KDP author, understanding Amazon's approach to copyright infringement is particularly important:

Reporting Infringement on Amazon

Amazon provides a specific process for reporting copyright infringement:

1. Visit the Amazon Infringement Reporting Form
2. Select the type of infringement (copyright, trademark, etc.)
3. Provide details about your work and the infringing content
4. Submit supporting documentation

Amazon typically responds within 1-2 business days and may remove infringing content while investigating.

Amazon's Content Review Process

When you report infringement:

1. Amazon reviews your claim and the allegedly infringing content
2. They may temporarily remove the reported content during investigation
3. The alleged infringer may be given an opportunity to respond
4. Amazon makes a determination based on the evidence provided

Protecting Your KDP Account

Be aware that false infringement claims can jeopardize your KDP account. Only report genuine infringement with clear evidence.

Content Disputes Between Authors

Amazon generally avoids adjudicating content disputes between authors when:

- Both claim to be the legitimate author
- The content is similar but not identical
- The dispute involves ideas rather than expression

In these cases, Amazon typically refers the parties to resolve the matter directly or through legal channels.

Technological Protection Measures

Several technological approaches can help protect your work:

Digital Watermarking

Digital watermarking embeds invisible identifiers in your ebook that:

- Survive format conversion and copying
- Can identify the source of leaked copies
- Provide evidence of ownership

Services like Digimarc and BooXtream offer digital watermarking for ebooks.

Digital Rights Management (DRM)

DRM technologies restrict how readers can use your ebook:

Pros of DRM:

- Makes casual copying more difficult
- Prevents easy sharing of files
- Gives authors a sense of control

Cons of DRM:

- Can frustrate legitimate readers
- May reduce sales
- Can be circumvented by determined pirates
- Locks readers into specific platforms

When publishing on KDP, you can choose whether to enable DRM. This decision should balance protection against reader experience and potential sales impact.

Blockchain and NFTs

Emerging technologies like blockchain and NFTs (Non-Fungible Tokens) offer new approaches to copyright protection:

- Blockchain registration: Services like Po.et and Binded allow you to timestamp and register your work on a blockchain, creating an immutable record of ownership.
- NFTs for books: Some authors are experimenting with NFTs to sell unique digital editions or special content,

creating additional revenue streams while establishing verifiable ownership records.

These technologies are still evolving but may offer additional protection options in the future.

Responding to Different Types of Infringement

Different types of infringement may require different responses:

For Counterfeit Print Books

1. Report directly to the marketplace (Amazon, eBay, etc.)
2. Provide evidence of your copyright ownership
3. Request immediate removal
4. Consider reporting to print-on-demand services if they're being used to create counterfeits

For Unauthorized Ebook Downloads

1. Send DMCA notices to the hosting website
2. If unsuccessful, escalate to the hosting provider
3. Submit removal requests to search engines to reduce visibility
4. Consider using automated monitoring and takedown services for widespread issues

For Content Scraping and Plagiarism

1. Document the similarities between your work and the infringing content
2. Contact the publisher or platform hosting the content
3. If the infringer is a fellow author, consider reaching out directly before escalation
4. Be prepared to demonstrate your work's earlier publication date

For Unauthorized Translations

1. Assert your translation rights (which are part of your copyright bundle)
2. Send takedown notices to platforms hosting unauthorized translations
3. Consider licensing official translations if there's genuine market interest

Building a Copyright Protection Strategy

An effective copyright protection strategy combines preventive measures, monitoring, and enforcement:

1. Preventive Measures

- Register your copyright for valuable works
- Include clear copyright notices in all formats
- Consider technological protections like watermarking

- Educate your readers about supporting authors through legitimate purchases

2. Regular Monitoring

- Set up automated monitoring tools
- Conduct periodic manual searches
- Stay connected with author communities for alerts
- Review major marketplaces regularly

3. Graduated Enforcement

- Focus on high-impact infringement first
- Use informal approaches (direct contact) when appropriate
- Escalate to formal DMCA notices when necessary
- Involve legal counsel for serious or persistent infringement

4. Documentation

- Maintain records of your copyright ownership
- Document all instances of infringement
- Keep copies of all notices sent and responses received
- Track the financial impact of significant infringement

Summary

Protecting your work from infringement requires vigilance and a strategic approach. By understanding the different types of infringement, implementing effective monitoring systems, and knowing how to use legal tools like DMCA takedown notices, you can significantly reduce unauthorized use of your work. Remember that perfect protection is impossible in the digital age. Focus your efforts on the most impactful cases of infringement, and balance protection measures against their costs in time, money, and reader experience. With a thoughtful approach to copyright protection, you can safeguard your creative investment while continuing to reach readers through legitimate channels.

In the next chapter, we'll explore copyright issues specific to Amazon's Kindle Direct Publishing platform, including KDP's terms of service, exclusivity considerations, and how Amazon's policies affect your rights as an author.

Chapter 7: Copyright Issues Specific to KDP

Amazon's Kindle Direct Publishing (KDP) platform has revolutionized self-publishing, allowing authors to reach millions of readers worldwide. However, publishing through KDP involves specific copyright considerations that differ from traditional publishing. This chapter explores KDP's terms of service, the rights you grant to Amazon, exclusivity considerations, territorial rights, and other copyright-related aspects unique to the KDP ecosystem.

KDP's Terms of Service Regarding Copyright

When you publish through KDP, you agree to Amazon's Terms of Service, which contain several important copyright-related provisions. Understanding these terms is essential for managing your rights effectively.

Copyright Ownership Assertion

KDP's terms require you to affirm that you either:

- Own the copyright to your book, or
- Have the necessary rights and permissions to publish it

This requirement appears straightforward, but it has significant implications:

1. You must be the legitimate rights holder: You cannot publish works to which you don't hold rights, including works by other authors (even if they're out of print) unless you've acquired those rights.

2. You need proper permissions: If your book includes third-party content (quotes, images, etc.), you must have obtained the necessary permissions.

3. You bear legal responsibility: If copyright disputes arise, Amazon may remove your book and hold you responsible for any legal consequences.

Rights You Grant to Amazon

When publishing through KDP, you grant Amazon specific rights to your work. These are not transfers of copyright ownership but rather licenses that allow Amazon to distribute and sell your book. The key rights you grant include:

1. Non-exclusive distribution rights: Amazon receives the right to reproduce, display, and distribute your book through their platforms.

2. Promotional rights: Amazon can use portions of your book (such as excerpts or the cover) for promotional purposes.

3. Format conversion rights: Amazon can convert your book into various formats compatible with their platforms and devices.

4. Territorial rights: Amazon can distribute your book in all territories where you've selected distribution rights.

5. Subsidiary rights for certain features: Rights to enable features like text-to-speech, lending, and snippets shown in search results.

It's important to note that these rights are non-exclusive (unless you enroll in KDP Select, which we'll discuss later), meaning you retain the ability to publish and distribute your work through other channels simultaneously.

Content Guidelines and Prohibited Content

KDP's Terms of Service also include content guidelines that can affect copyright matters:

1. Public domain works: Amazon has specific requirements for publishing public domain works, which we'll explore later in this chapter.

2. Plagiarism prohibition: KDP explicitly prohibits plagiarism, which includes copying substantial portions of others' works without permission.

3. Content that infringes others' intellectual property: This includes unauthorized use of trademarked characters, settings from other authors' works, or fan fiction based on copyrighted works.

4. Content that impersonates other authors or brands: Creating works that might confuse readers about authorship or association with known brands.

Violations of these guidelines can result in removal of your books, withholding of royalties, or termination of your KDP account.

KDP Select and Exclusivity Considerations

KDP Select is Amazon's optional program that provides additional benefits in exchange for digital exclusivity. This program has significant copyright implications that authors should carefully consider.

What Is KDP Select?

KDP Select is a program that offers several benefits:

- Inclusion in Kindle Unlimited (KU) and the Kindle Owners' Lending Library (KOLL)
- Access to promotional tools like Free Book Promotions and Kindle Countdown Deals
- Higher royalty rates in certain territories
- Increased visibility on Amazon's platform

In exchange, you grant Amazon exclusive distribution rights for the digital version of your book for 90-day periods (automatically renewing unless you opt out).

Copyright Implications of KDP Select

The exclusivity requirement has several important copyright implications:

1. Limited exercise of your distribution rights: While enrolled in KDP Select, you cannot distribute the digital version of your book through any other channel, including:

   - Other ebook retailers (Barnes & Noble, Apple Books, Kobo, etc.)
   - Your own website
   - Email newsletters
   - Subscription services like Scribd or Bookfunnel

2. Print and audio rights unaffected: The exclusivity applies only to the digital (ebook) version. You can still sell print books and audiobooks through any channel.

3. Temporary nature of the restriction: The exclusivity is for 90-day periods, after which you can choose not to renew and regain full distribution rights.

4. Potential contract conflicts: If you have existing contracts with other distributors, enrolling in KDP Select could create contractual conflicts.

Strategic Copyright Considerations for KDP Select

When deciding whether to enroll in KDP Select, consider these copyright-related factors:

1. Market reach vs. exclusivity: Weigh the benefits of broader distribution against the advantages of Amazon's exclusive programs.

2. Rights segmentation strategy: Consider using KDP Select strategically for some titles while keeping others widely distributed.

3. Time-limited exclusivity: Use the 90-day periods strategically, perhaps launching with KDP Select before expanding to other platforms.

4. Series strategy: Some authors keep the first book in a series in KDP Select as a reader acquisition tool while distributing later books widely.

Public Domain Works on KDP

Publishing public domain works on KDP involves specific considerations and requirements. Amazon has implemented policies to prevent the proliferation of low-quality public domain titles and ensure value for readers.

Amazon's Public Domain Content Guidelines

If you're publishing a public domain work on KDP, Amazon requires that your edition provide additional value beyond the basic text. According to their guidelines, your version must include at least one of the following:

1. Original content: Such as annotations, illustrations, or commentary
2. Translations: New or unique translations of the original work
3. Formatting improvements: Enhanced typography, navigation, or organization

Simply republishing a public domain text without adding value may result in your book being removed from the platform.

Copyright Notice for Public Domain Works

When publishing public domain works with your own additions, your copyright page should clearly distinguish between:

- The public domain content (not protected by copyright)
- Your original contributions (protected by your copyright)

Example copyright notice:

```
The original text of [Title] by [Original
Author] is in the public domain.
Introduction, annotations, and
illustrations © 2025 [Your Name]. All
rights reserved.
```

Avoiding Misleading Copyright Claims

Be careful not to claim copyright over the entire work if you've only added minimal original content to a public domain text. Misleading copyright claims can lead to:

- Removal of your book from KDP
- Potential legal issues
- Damage to your reputation as an author

International Considerations for Public Domain Works

Remember that copyright duration varies by country (as discussed in Chapter 4). A work might be in the public domain in the United States but still protected in other countries. When publishing through KDP's global distribution, you need to consider the copyright status in all territories where you plan to distribute.

Metadata and Copyright Information

The metadata you provide when publishing on KDP has important copyright implications:

Publication Date

The publication date you enter in KDP:

- Creates a public record of when your work was first published
- Can be important for establishing copyright priority in disputes
- Affects copyright duration in some jurisdictions

For new works, use the actual date of first publication. For previously published works, use the original publication date, not the KDP republication date.

Author Name and Contributors

The author name and contributor information you provide:

- Establishes attribution for copyright purposes
- Should accurately reflect the creators involved
- Can include pseudonyms, but Amazon may require verification of your identity

If you're publishing under a pen name, you can list your pseudonym as the author while maintaining your legal name on your KDP account for payment and tax purposes.

ISBN Information

While not strictly a copyright matter, ISBN information relates to your book's identity:

- If you use Amazon's free ISBN, Amazon is listed as the publisher of record

- If you use your own ISBN, you or your publishing company is listed as the publisher
- This affects who controls certain aspects of your book's metadata in industry databases

Territorial Rights and Distribution

KDP allows you to select the territories where your book will be available, which has copyright implications:

Territorial Rights Selection

When publishing on KDP, you can choose:

- Worldwide rights: Your book is available in all Amazon marketplaces
- Individual territories: You select specific countries or regions

This selection should align with the territorial rights you actually hold. For example, if you've licensed the rights to your book to a publisher in certain countries, you should exclude those territories from your KDP distribution.

Copyright Enforcement Across Territories

Different territories have varying approaches to copyright enforcement:

- Some countries have robust copyright protection systems

- Others have limited enforcement mechanisms
- Digital piracy rates vary significantly by region

Consider these factors when deciding on your territorial distribution strategy.

Translation Rights

KDP distribution does not automatically include translation rights. If your book gains popularity in non-English markets, you might receive interest from:

- Foreign publishers seeking translation rights
- Amazon itself through Amazon Crossing (their translation publishing program)

Carefully evaluate any translation rights offers, as they represent a separate set of rights from your original language publication.

Content Updates and Copyright Implications

KDP allows you to update your book's content after publication, which has several copyright considerations:

Copyright Date for Updated Works

When you make substantial updates to your book:

- You might want to update the copyright notice to reflect the new version
- A common format is "© 2023, 2025 [Your Name]" showing both original and update years
- Major revisions might warrant registering the new version with the Copyright Office

Notifying Existing Customers

Amazon may allow you to notify existing customers about significant updates:

- This feature is typically reserved for major content changes, not minor corrections
- Customers can choose to receive the updated version
- This helps ensure readers have the most current version of your work

Version Tracking

For significant revisions, consider:

- Noting the version or edition number on the copyright page
- Maintaining a version history for your own records
- Documenting major changes between versions

This practice helps track the evolution of your copyright-protected content and can be valuable if disputes arise.

Rights Reversion and Termination

Understanding how to terminate your agreement with KDP and regain your rights is an important aspect of copyright management:

Removing Your Book from KDP

You can remove your book from KDP at any time by:

1. Going to your KDP Bookshelf
2. Selecting the book you want to unpublish
3. Choosing "Unpublish" from the available options

This action:

- Removes your book from sale on Amazon
- Terminates Amazon's license to distribute your work
- May take up to 72 hours to fully process

KDP Select Termination

If your book is enrolled in KDP Select:

- You cannot remove it from KDP until the current 90-day enrollment period ends
- You can choose not to auto-renew KDP Select
- After the enrollment period ends, you regain full distribution rights

Rights After Termination

After terminating your agreement with KDP:

- Amazon retains no rights to publish or distribute your work
- You are free to publish elsewhere
- Amazon may continue to display bibliographic information about your book
- Customers who purchased your book while it was available retain their copies

Account Termination and Copyright Issues

In some cases, Amazon may terminate a KDP account due to violations of their terms of service. This situation raises several copyright concerns:

Rights After Account Termination

If Amazon terminates your KDP account:

- Your books will be removed from the Amazon store
- You retain your copyright ownership
- You can publish your works through other channels
- You may lose access to your KDP dashboard and reports

Proving Ownership After Termination

If you need to prove ownership of your works after account termination:

- Your copyright registration (if you registered) remains valid
- Your original manuscripts and documentation remain important evidence
- Publication metadata from other platforms can help establish your rights

Appealing Account Termination

If your account was terminated due to copyright-related issues:

- You can appeal Amazon's decision
- Provide evidence of your copyright ownership
- Address any specific violations cited by Amazon
- Consider seeking legal assistance if significant royalties or rights are at stake

Copyright Disputes on KDP

Amazon has specific procedures for handling copyright disputes between authors or publishers:

Infringement Reporting Process

If you believe another KDP author has infringed your copyright:

1. Use Amazon's infringement reporting form (www.amazon.com/report/infringement)
2. Provide specific details about your work and the alleged infringement
3. Include evidence supporting your claim

Amazon will investigate and may:

- Remove the infringing content
- Contact the alleged infringer for their response
- Make a determination based on the evidence provided

Responding to Infringement Claims

If your KDP book is accused of copyright infringement:

1. You'll receive notification from Amazon
2. Your book may be temporarily removed during investigation
3. You'll have an opportunity to respond with evidence supporting your rights
4. Amazon will make a determination based on the evidence

Responding promptly and with clear evidence is crucial to resolving such disputes favorably.

When Amazon Won't Intervene

Amazon generally avoids adjudicating certain types of disputes:

- Claims of idea theft (since ideas aren't copyrightable)
- Disputes between collaborators or co-authors
- Complex ownership disputes requiring court resolution

In these cases, Amazon typically refers the parties to resolve the matter through legal channels.

Best Practices for Copyright Management on KDP

Based on the considerations discussed in this chapter, here are best practices for managing your copyright effectively on KDP:

1. Maintain Clear Documentation

- Keep original manuscripts and drafts with timestamps
- Document your creative process
- Save correspondence related to your work
- Maintain records of publication dates and versions

2. Be Strategic About Rights

- Consider carefully whether KDP Select exclusivity makes sense for your work
- Make informed decisions about territorial rights

- Think strategically about translation rights and other subsidiary rights

3. Understand Your Agreement

- Read and understand KDP's Terms of Service
- Stay informed about policy changes
- Know what rights you're granting and what rights you retain

4. Monitor Your Work

- Regularly search for unauthorized copies of your KDP books
- Check for similar titles or content that might infringe your rights
- Use Amazon's tools to report any infringement you discover

5. Maintain Professional Relationships

- Respond professionally to copyright disputes
- Work collaboratively with Amazon when issues arise
- Consider the long-term implications of copyright enforcement actions

Su nmary

Publ shing through KDP involves navigating specific copyright cons iderations unique to Amazon's ecosystem. By understanding KDP's terms of service, the rights you grant to Amazon, exclusivity considerations, and other platform-specific issues, you can make informed decisions about how to manage and protect your intellectual property.

Remember that while Amazon provides the platform, you remain the copyright owner of your work. Making strategic choices about how you license your rights through KDP can significantly impact your book's reach, your revenue potential, and your long-term control over your creative work.

In the next chapter, we'll explore special copyright considerations for different types of books, including fiction, non-fiction, illustrated works, and compilations.

Conclusion: Navigating Copyright Law as a Self-Published Author

Throughout this guide, we've explored the multifaceted world of copyright law as it applies to self-published authors on Amazon's Kindle Direct Publishing platform. From understanding the fundamental principles of copyright protection to navigating the specific requirements of KDP, you now have a comprehensive foundation for managing your intellectual property rights effectively.

Key Takeaways

Let's review the most important points from each chapter:

Copyright Fundamentals

- Copyright protection is automatic upon creation of your work
- Copyright gives you exclusive rights to reproduce, distribute, display, perform, and create derivatives of your work
- Copyright protects the expression of ideas, not the ideas themselves
- Copyright lasts for your lifetime plus 70 years in most cases

Copyright Registration

- While registration isn't required for protection, it provides significant legal advantages
- Registration is necessary before filing an infringement lawsuit in the U.S.

- Registering before infringement (or within three months of publication) makes you eligible for statutory damages and attorney's fees
- The registration process is straightforward and can be completed online

Creating an Effective Copyright Page

- A proper copyright page includes a copyright notice, rights reserved statement, and relevant disclaimers
- Different types of books require different copyright page elements
- Your copyright page serves both legal and informational purposes
- While not legally required, a well-crafted copyright page is a professional standard

International Copyright Considerations

- The Berne Convention provides automatic protection in over 180 countries
- Copyright duration and enforcement vary significantly by country
- International rights management becomes increasingly important as your career grows
- Translation rights represent a valuable subset of your copyright bundle

Using Others' Work in Your Book

- Fair use allows limited use of copyrighted material without permission under specific circumstances
- When in doubt about fair use, seek permission
- Public domain works can be freely used, but verify their status carefully
- Proper citation is an ethical requirement regardless of copyright status

Protecting Your Work from Infringement

- Monitor for unauthorized use through various tools and strategies
- DMCA takedown notices provide an effective mechanism for removing infringing content
- Focus your enforcement efforts on high-impact infringement
- Balance protection measures against their costs in time, money, and reader experience

Copyright Issues Specific to KDP

- KDP's terms of service grant Amazon specific, non-exclusive rights to distribute your work
- KDP Select requires digital exclusivity in exchange for additional benefits

- Amazon has specific requirements for publishing public domain works
- You retain your copyright when publishing through KDP and can terminate the agreement

Best Practices for Copyright Management

Based on everything we've covered, here are the essential best practices for managing your copyright as a self-published author:

1. Protect Your Work Proactively

- Register your copyright for valuable works
- Include proper copyright notices in all your books
- Keep records of your creative process and publication dates
- Consider technological measures like digital watermarking for high-value content

2. Respect Others' Rights

- Obtain necessary permissions for third-party content
- Understand the limitations of fair use
- Properly attribute sources even when permission isn't required
- Verify the status of supposedly public domain works

3. Make Informed Business Decisions

- Understand the rights you grant to platforms like KDP
- Consider the trade-offs of programs like KDP Select
- Think strategically about international and subsidiary rights
- Balance copyright protection against reader experience and market reach

4. Be Prepared for Problems

- Monitor for unauthorized use of your work
- Know how to send effective DMCA takedown notices
- Document infringement when it occurs
- Understand when to handle issues yourself and when to seek legal help

5. Stay Informed

- Copyright law and platform policies evolve over time
- Join author communities to share information and experiences
- Follow reliable sources for updates on copyright issues
- Review platform terms of service when they change

When to Seek Professional Help

While this guide provides a solid foundation, certain situations warrant professional legal assistance:

- Complex permissions or licensing arrangements
- Significant infringement of your work
- International rights management
- Contract negotiations for subsidiary rights
- Copyright registration for unusual or complex works
- Disputes with platforms or other authors

In these cases, consulting with an intellectual property attorney experienced in publishing matters can be a worthwhile investment.

Final Thoughts

Copyright law exists to protect creative expression and encourage the creation of new works. As a self-published author, understanding copyright empowers you to:

- Protect your creative investment
- Make informed business decisions
- Navigate publishing platforms effectively
- Build on others' work legally and ethically
- Create a sustainable career as an author

The digital publishing landscape continues to evolve, presenting both challenges and opportunities for copyright management. By applying the principles and practices outlined in this guide, you'll be well-equipped to protect your rights while reaching readers around the world.

Remember that copyright is ultimately about balancing protection with purpose. Your work deserves protection, but the ultimate goal is to share your stories, ideas, and knowledge with readers. Finding the right balance between protecting your rights and connecting with your audience is the key to long-term success as a self-published author.

We wish you the best of luck in your publishing journey!

Thank You for Checking out my Book! If interested, Please check out my Author page, Have a fabulous day! Link Here - https://www.amazon.com/author/paigeharg is - *Paige Hargis*

Printed in Dunstable, United Kingdom